Bird Banding
with an Audubon Naturalist

Northern Flicker

George J Robinson Ph.D.

Published by: EnviroScribes
Mahopac, New York

ISBN: 10: 1492176117
ISBN-13: 978-1492176114

CONTENTS

Acknowledgments

1   Why Band Birds   Pg. 1

2   Getting Ready   Pg. 2

3   Catching the Birds   Pg. 5

4   Male or Female   Pg. 14

5   Age   Pg. 18

6   Banding   Pg. 21

7   Weighing   Pg. 22

8   Release   Pg. 24

Acknowledgments

It takes a dedicated person to begin banding birds at 5 am and work till noon. That's why I must give special thanks to the Bedford Audubon Society who conducted these bird banding sessions. This book would not be possible without the expertise of these naturalists: Tait Johansson, Alec Nelson, Benjamin Van Doren and Victoria Watson.

Yellow Throat

Scarlet Tanager

Can you tell what type of bird this is? Whether it is a male or female? Its size? Its weight? Its habitat? Where it's been or where it's going?

These are the questions a scientist asks during a bird banding session. The answers enable researchers to study the migratory patterns of various bird populations.

Starting at dawn, the bird banding team treks through the 318 acre Parker-Hunter Memorial Sanctuary in Westchester County, New York. After setting up their banding station, they slough through mud, over logs and stone walls to unfurl their nets for the day's catch.

The nets are made of nylon and are about forty feet long and six feet high. The team places the nets in different **habitats**. One area is a red maple swamp; another area is a dry mixed-**deciduous** (leaf dropping) forest.

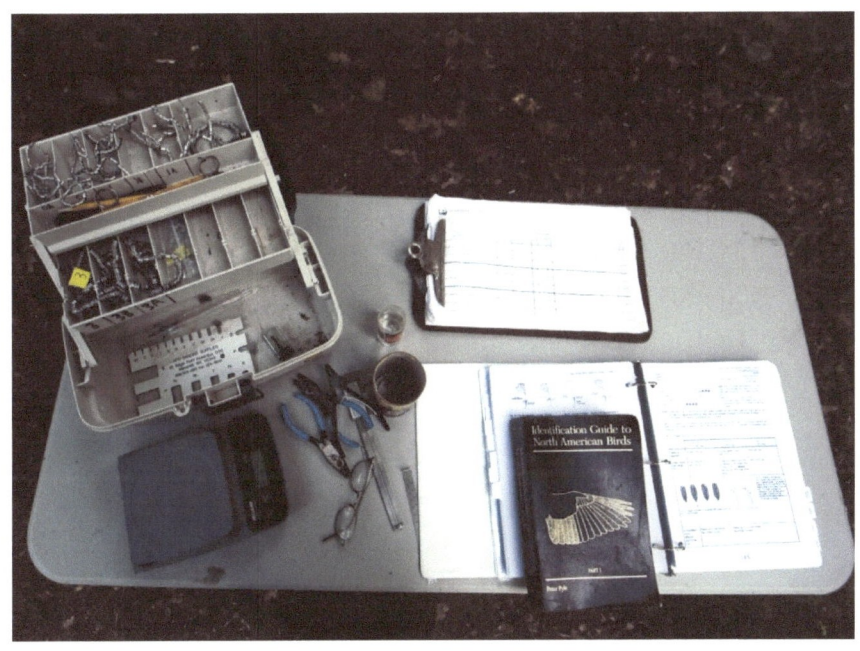

The official bird banding station is simply a folding table set within walking distance of the sites. The tools are few but usually include: a tackle box with different size bands, crimping pliers, a ruler, a scale, a can, a bird identification book and data charts.

Once an hour the team makes the one-half mile circuit to retrieve the birds snagged in each of the ten nets that have been set out.

Then they enter the information into a **National Database** for research on population studies. For example, researchers might want to know how many wood thrushes returned from Central America, or how many veeries made the trip back from South America.

Wood Thrush

The team must take care in disentangling the birds from the nets. Gentle but firm hands hold the birds while the net is removed. They must free the head first, followed by the wings and finally, the legs.

Sometimes the bird holds on tight with its talons and won't let go. So the handler releases some pressure on the bird's body which tricks the bird into thinking it can fly away and so lets go of the net.

Then they carry the bird back to the field office in the most humane way possible: in a breathable cloth sack.

A clothes pin is attached to the sack to identify the net and the habitat the bird was caught in.

Wood Thrush

Some birds already have a band on their legs with an **identification number**. Then the naturalist notes the number on a data sheet. This information will be useful to researchers tracking bird migration.

In addition to the band number, the ornithologist writes down the bird's species, sex, age, size and weight. To help with the identification, the field worker refers to a guide book of North American birds written by **Dr. Peter Pyle.**

Plumage is the first thing a naturalist looks at to identify whether the bird is a male or a female. Usually, the more colorful the bird's feathers are, the more likely it is a male. For example, the male cardinal has bright red feathers while the female is a muted brown.

Likewise, the male downy woodpecker has a small red patch on the nape of its head while the female does not.

To determine if a bird is female, the ornithologist looks for a **brood patch** (used to incubate the eggs).

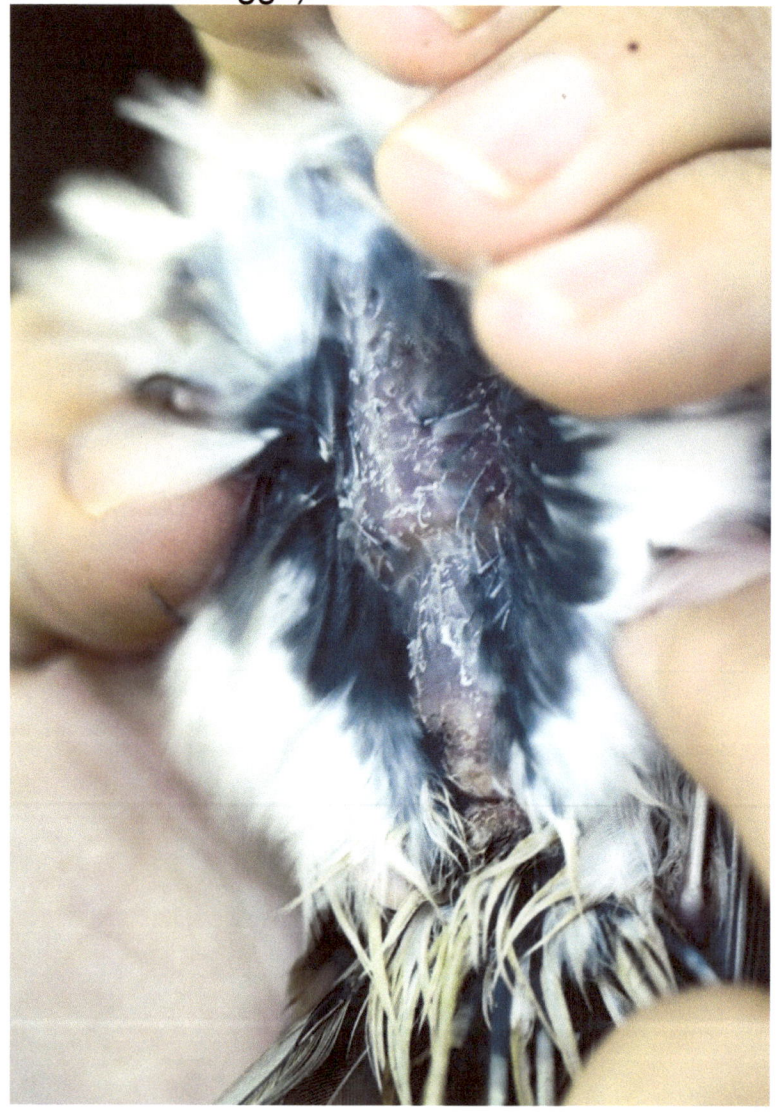

If there is a large **cloacal protuberance** (a tube for transferring semen), the bird is a male.

A bird's age is recorded as either in its **hatch year** (the year it was born) or after its hatch year. One way to determine age is to push back the head feathers to see to what extent the secondary covering over the skull has hardened. This bone formation is called **ossification**.

A fully formed bone structure indicates the bird is past its hatch year.

Downy Woodpecker

Another way to determine the age of the bird is to look at the **primary covert feathers** which are placed over the long flight feathers. If the primary covert feathers are sharp and pointed, the bird has young new feathers. If they are rounded and abraded, the bird has older used feathers.

The naturalist uses a **wing ruler** to measure the length of the wing from the shoulder to the tip. In order to ensure a standardized measurement, the field worker makes sure not to press on the wing. If necessary, wing measurement could help identify sex and age, but it is most often used to measure growth. This measurement is also used to chart the size variability of the species.

Northern Flicker

Each species of bird requires a specific sized metal band. For example, a small bird like a gnatcatcher would need an 0A band while a large pileated woodpecker would need a size 04.The bird bander uses a crimping tool to attach the circular band to the leg of the bird. He then records the identification number on the data sheet.

Weighing a finicky bird who wants to escape requires an unique but simple solution. The field biologist places the bird inside a juice can and covers the top of the can with his hands. Then he can easily place the can on the scale. To calculate the total weight of the bird, the biologist simply subtracts the can's weight in grams from the total.

Before he releases the Scarlet Tanager, Tait Johansson, the Audubon Naturalist, takes a digital photograph to have a visual documentation of the bird for the National Database.

When all the data has been collected, the bird is set free. It may be recaptured again in the same area or somewhere along its migratory journey. If it is, this new information will be entered into the National Database for researchers to use.

Northern Flicker

For more information about birding and bird banding go to these **web sites**:

Ebird.org

Bird.cornel.edu

Birdpop.org/maps.htm

Birding.about.com

Audubon.org

ABOUT THE AUTHOR

Dr. George Robinson grew up in the Bronx and discovered nature in its pocket parks and in the estuaries of the Hudson River. He is an educator, school administrator and nature photographer. He has led student expeditions to Key Largo to research the coral reef and has photographed the diverse bird population of the Everglades. Dr. Robinson especially loves to photograph the ecosystems surrounding his home in the Hudson Valley and in the National Parks.

Other EBooks by Dr. Robinson

ABC's of the Coral Reef

El ABC's de los Arrecifes de Coral

www.ingramcontent.com/pod-product-compliance
Lightning Source LLC
Chambersburg PA
CBHW050927290526
45792CB00002B/910